T0148558

SPIRITUAL ABUSE

Learning and
overcoming spiritual
abuse in the church
and home

Yvonne Davis-Weir

WESTBOW*
PRESS
A DIVISION OF THOMAS NELSON
& ZONDERVAN

WestBow Press books may be ordered through booksellers or by contacting:

WestBow Press
A Division of Thomas Nelson & Zondervan
1663 Liberty Drive
Bloomington, IN 47403
www.westbowpress.com
1 (866) 928-1240

Because of the dynamic nature of the Internet, any web addresses or
links contained in this book may have changed since publication and
may no longer be valid. The views expressed in this work are solely those
of the author and do not necessarily reflect the views of the publisher,
and the publisher hereby disclaims any responsibility for them.

Any people depicted in stock imagery provided by Thinkstock are models,
and such images are being used for illustrative purposes only.
Certain stock imagery © Thinkstock.

ISBN: 978-1-4908-7727-3 (sc)
ISBN: 978-1-4908-7728-0 (e)

Library of Congress Control Number: 2015906010

Print information available on the last page.

WestBow Press rev. date: 4/21/2015

Contents

Foreword

The topic of spiritual abuse is a relatively new one. We have all probably heard of physical abuse and even emotional abuse, but most have never heard of spiritual abuse. In this book, Yvonne Weir deciphers the different layers associated with this kind of abuse.

I met Yvonne Weir a few years back when I was teaching a college writing class at Trinity International University. All of the students were assigned topics for a final essay project which would be due at the end of the class. In conversations with Yvonne the topic of spiritual abuse came up, and she decided that she would research this topic further. I believe it was the Holy Spirit that, through the research, sparked something in Yvonne to want to know and do something about spiritual abuse. As you will read in the following pages, this kind of abuse shatters the very essence of our relationship with God. Yvonne explores in depth how the Scriptures can be used and distorted to hurt and control others.

The Bible provides us with tools to use in our daily lives to develop a godly relationship and find our identity in Christ—essential to our walk as Christians.

Yvonne Weir has become one of the most beloved students around campus. Her diligence and desire to learn are contagious. Throughout the book she exhorts readers to stay totally grounded in our Lord Jesus Christ, fully armored and ready for battle. The Bible states that Jesus committed no sin yet suffered a death which is the consequence or wages of sin. By becoming human, Jesus became subject to the possibility and actuality of death. In his resurrection, Jesus left behind the conditions associated with life on this earth. Thus the pain, both physical and psychological, of earth is no longer his. We need to have a profound appreciation for the full measure of what Christ did to bring us into fellowship with the Father. May this book shed light and bring awareness about spiritual abuse, as well as bring healing to its victims.

> "My lips will shout for joy, when I sing praises to you; my soul also, which you have redeemed" (Psalm 71:16, ESV).

—Professor Stephanie Santana

Acknowledgments

First and foremost, I would like to give honor to the Holy Spirit, the head of my life, for equipping me with the wisdom to write this book and the endurance and patience to complete it.

I would like to thank my family for their continued love and support. I also thank them for the many days and nights when they assumed the responsibilities in the home while I worked on writing this, as well as my other books. Included in this wonderful bunch are my mom, Edith, my dad, Melbourne (deceased), and my children, Michael, Linval, Sasha, Carlton (CJ), Samantha, and Clifford. Also my dear sisters, Maureen Dwyer, Sharon and her husband Eli Moore (living in Jamaica), and Hyacinth Dennis (now deceased). They have always been my inspiration, and this achievement would not be possible without them.

I would like to salute Trinity International University in Davie for making the writing of this book possible. In whatever one chooses to undertake in life, one will always require the help and support of others. In my case I can proudly say that Trinity International University has taught me a lot. As a result of this educational nurturing, I was inspired to write my first book. As a student of this prestigious university for several years, I have improved, both as a person and as a pastor. I also learned how to effectively prepare my Sunday morning sermons so that the people of God may be adequately fed. It is through this great knowledge and wonderful experience at Trinity International University that this book *Spiritual Abuse? What Is That?* was born. It is my intention that whoever reads this book will not only learn about spiritual abuse, but will in turn educate others about its existence.

I also applaud the following people who play very important roles in my life: Professor Stephanie Santana at Trinity International University, who instigated and helped inspire me to write this book; Pastor Holly Farver at Potential Church; Dr. Patricia Colangelo at Trinity International University; Dr. Ralph Curtin at Trinity International University; Dr. Steve Doan and Dr. Norman Wise; Dr. G. Cohen; Professor Art Bailey; Professor D. Reid; all professors at Trinity International University.

I also thank the late, great Pastor Emanuel Flemmings; Pastor Winston Nelson at Apostolic Faith Rescue Mission; Pastor Doreen McTaggart at Mount Olive Pentecostal; Bishop Shane Paisley, who is responsible for my pastoral ordination; Ms. Faye Ralph, who introduced me and my family to Trinity International University; Natalie Evans; Gretta Marshall; Ashdale Thomas; Missionary Paulette Dunkley; Beryl Francis; Herbert Cooper.

Nothing would be possible without these wonderful people making positive differences in my life. Today I am surviving academically because of their words and deeds of encouragement over the years. As a result of the seeds they've sown in me, this book has grown into a big, fruitful tree, and many people will be fed as a result.

I am also pleased to acknowledge my friends and family on Face book. I remember on many occasions when I experienced those *down* days, I would drop in on my friends and family, and they would always have a cheerful word waiting for me. They are always praying for me and posting uplifting words and special prayers on my page.

There are so many more wonderful people whom I want to mention, but time and space do not allow me to do so. But always remember, I love and appreciate you.

Testimonials and Endorsements

Yvonne Weir's personal experience with spiritual abuse speaks volumes ... even louder than the resources quoted by her in this work. Her combined insight and advice gives great credence to this problem that haunts the corporate church today, and her counsel will aid in the healing process of many who have been injured by this form of mistreatment, often inflicted by misguided leaders believing they are speaking for God.

—Dr. Ralph D. Curtin

★ ★ ★ ★ ★ ★

Spiritual abuse is a real issue today as it was in the early days of the church. Yvonne Weir covers the many Scriptures that warn us to guard against this issue. This is so helpful to those who may be struggling with it and need to know where in the Scriptures to find guidance.

—Dr. Patricia L. Colangelo

★ ★ ★ ★ ★ ★

Spiritual abuse is one of the many topics that is not talked or preached about. God has blessed and inspired Pastor Yvonne Weir to expose this evil and bring to light the damaging effect of spiritual abuse. She is unsurpassed in her quest for knowledge; her desire is to edify, educate, and expose this evil. This book meets a need that has been lacking for some time in the church and the world. I am fully convinced that this book is ordained by God. It will impact your life and change your perception about this evil spirit that is under cover in the body of Christ. It is a must-read for all. You will not be able to put it down once you start reading it. Make this book the newest addition to your library. Read it and re-read it with an open heart, and encourage others to do the same. May the Lord bless you; may the Holy Spirit equip and lead you and enable you to help others to be free from this deadly evil of spiritual abuse.

—Winston E. Nelson, author and pastor of
Apostolic Faith Rescue Mission, Miami, FL

* * * * * * *

I am grateful for the friendship that God has given me through Yvonne Weir. I know that, as believers, God does not allow anything to pass through our hands (whether good or bad) that He cannot use for His glory. I pray for this text and the insight that it will bring to all those who seek Him. God's intention is always covered in all His love and grace and it opens our eyes to the truth of His Word. May we stay humbled and surrendered to know that God's desire is never to have any man or woman use His Word and His church to harm others. May we walk in His love, grace, and truth, not in our own interpretations.

—Holly Farver, pastor of Potential Church, Cooper City

Introduction

Spiritual abuse? Hmm … You probably think that sounds crazy. You might also think that this is something that was made up. But it is not a funny game; it is more than having a headache, taking painkillers, going to bed, and feeling better the next day. It is much more than a mere feeling. Some of you may be so sure that this is something that cannot be substantiated. We've all heard about physical abuse, verbal abuse, emotional abuse, and even financial abuse, but spiritual abuse is rarely heard of and very seldom discussed.

One of the dangers of spiritual abuse is that the signs are not as visible as in physical abuse. I liken spiritual abuse to a large, infested sore. Instead of sewing up the spiritual sutures of abuse by applying the necessary dressings for healing, we tend to cover the disgrace with a Band-Aid, thinking it will heal and go away unnoticed. But instead of healing, the wound festers and eventually erupts into a large wound. This is what happens when spiritual abuse is ignored; this is what happens when Satan commands his demons to infiltrate our homes and churches. And as a result, the little blister has festered into something much worse and is out of control. Spiritual abuse is in the church and in the home. It is here, it is real, it is sin, and it hurts.

This book is written not only to help those who are experiencing the abuse, but also for those who are responsible for the abuse. It intends to let them know that God is watching. Just as problems in marriages are caused by infidelity and other things, in the same way relationships are negatively affected by this type of exploitation. The Lord is obviously not pleased with people who delight themselves in abusing His children, especially those whom He placed in authority and to whom He gave the wisdom to help others. "At times even some Christian counselors write-off true victims of Spiritual Abuse as being more victims of their own thin skin than anything else. They dismiss the horrific accounts of these victims as being "too subjective" to be reliable. In some Christian circles, it has become standard operating procedure to automatically file the claims of Spiritual Abuse under the heading of mere 'perception of Spiritual Abuse" (Henzel, R., 2014, p. 2). This is aimed especially at those who are in higher authority and who are held to certain standards, such as those who are responsible for nurturing His children. First Peter 5:2–3 says, "Be shepherds of God's flock that is under your care, watching over them--not because you must, but because you are willing, as God wants you to be; not pursuing dishonest gain, but eager to serve." Mark 10:42–44 also says, "Jesus called them together and said, 'You know that those who are regarded as rulers of the Gentiles lord it over them, and their high officials exercise authority over them. Not so with you. Instead, whoever wants to become great among you must be your servant, and whoever wants to be first must be slave of all'" (ESV).

Some of us have come in contact with these spirits of abuse at one time or another, whether we are white or black, rich or poor, Christian or non-Christian. In fact, some of us are daily living in obnoxious and intolerable conditions with this demon. So then, what is spiritual abuse, and where did it come from?

Sounds confusing, right? Don't be confused; you are not alone.

Before you read any farther, I think it is important to pray and ask God to give you wisdom, guidance, and understanding as you read; pray that your eyes will be opened to the effects of spiritual abuse.

Heavenly Father, we come to You in no other name but in the name of Your Son, who selflessly gave His life for our sakes. I pray that as Your children read this book on spiritual abuse, they will be equipped with the wisdom needed to fight evil forces that try to overtake them on a daily basis. Lord, help them to be strong soldiers in Your army as they march to war. I also pray that this book will enlighten everyone who reads it, and they will help others who are struggling in this and other areas. We daily seek Your face for guidance because, without You, we are all vulnerable and helpless. Continue to strengthen, guide, and bless us as we humble ourselves before you each day. These things we ask in Your holy name. Amen.

CHAPTER 1

Defining Spiritual Abuse

What is spiritual abuse? Just as emotional abuse affects one emotionally while physical abuse inflicts pain and bodily injury on its victim, spiritual abuse affects one spiritually. It is the result of a spiritual leader or system that tries to control, manipulate, or dominate person. This control is often in the form of fear. This is considered a major factor in mind control/coercive persuasion or thought reform. There are those who feel the latter come into play in cases such as these, while others feel the thinking is in error. Regardless of where one stands on this, it does not lessen the effects of spiritual abuse. —Lois Gibson

Spiritual abuse occurs when any spiritual leader misuses his or her authority. In some cases this abuse can be intentional when that person tries to dominate others in the name of Jesus. In other instances it can be something that was passed down from one leader to the next. In some circumstances where tradition is involved, the rules and regulations are automatically transferred with no questions asked.

Orbit Epstein, Joseph Schwartz, and Rachel Schwartz also say, "Spiritual abuse is the enforcement of a position of power, leadership or attachment in which total unquestioning obedience in thought, word or action, is demanded of a child, adolescent or adult under threat of punishment in this life and in any afterlife for themselves, their families, helpers or others."

There are so many different ways to describe this spiritual disease. In any case it is real, and as a result, many people are silently suffering from it.

It is an act of Satan when we go into God's house feeling broken and disheartened and leave feeling worse than when we went in. "Ask yourself if you are in a place of worship where there is always a fresh, radical presentation of the freedom and equality of individual followers of Christ. If not, consider leaving, because in the end you will find your Christian community was never really about Christ or His people at all" (Wade Burleson). It is also the work of the Devil when Christians who are supposed to be living in loving homes feel ostracized because the head of the house displays actions contrary to God's commands. So whether we are at home, in the church, or even on the street, there are no places to hide.

> "Spiritual Abuse communicates the message that God does not love and accept us as we are, and that we must work to earn God's approval also that God's love and grace are not enough. Once the devaluing messages of spiritual abuse become internalized, we start to live as if the messages were true, and this inevitably leads us to pass abusive messages to others."

Many Christians are living in spiritually abusive situations and are not even aware of it. They become so convinced that their lifestyles are aligned with the Word of God that nothing you say to them will change their minds. My prayer is that after reading this book, they will come to the realization that their standards of living are far from being God-ordained. J. Van Vonderen says, "Spiritual abuse is always a power issue. In order for abuse to happen by definition, it has to come from a place of higher power to a place of lesser power. People in lower power positions can't abuse people in higher power."

It is important for us as believers to be alert to the things that are not of God and warn others of these problems and how to avoid them. It is not easy to identify spiritual abuse because this disease disguises itself in such cunning ways that even the host is not aware of its existence. The ones who recognize it enjoy its company so much that they refuse any forms of treatment, therapy, or cure. Many church leaders feel they can hide behind their pulpits, robes, and expensive suits as they physically, emotionally, and mentally insult God's children, but God is certainly not pleased.

As Christian leaders we must not be too free or quick to use phrases such as, "Thus says the Lord" or "The Lord gave me a word for you." Like I said previously, if the Lord did not tell you to say it, don't say it. The Scripture says, "Beloved, believe not every spirit, but try the spirits whether they are of God: because many false prophets are gone out into the world" (1 John 4:1 NIV). Second Peter 2:1 adds, "But there were false prophets also among the people, even as there shall be false teachers among you, who privily shall bring in damnable heresies, even denying the Lord that bought them, and bring upon themselves swift destruction."

All God wants us to do is to give the Word exactly as He instructs us—no more, no less. He does not want us to add salt, sugar, water, ketchup, or barbeque sauce—no altering of His Word. If we do, there will be terrible consequences because, as a result of our selfish and sinful acts, many people will be led astray. It is always a terrible thing when the wrath of God comes upon us. There are many stories in the Bible of leaders who added on to God's instructions, and as a result, they suffered the consequences. Some recovered, like King David, as evidenced in Psalm 32:5: "Then I acknowledged my sin to you and did not cover up my iniquity. I said, 'I will confess my transgressions to the LORD. And you forgave the guilt of my sin'" (NIV). This Scripture shows David reflecting on the wrong things he did and how he sought help by going to the Lord for forgiveness. Then there was King Saul, who did not get a second chance to redeem himself because he took matters in his own hands. According to 1 Samuel 13:11–14, he did the following:

> What have you done?" asked Samuel. Saul replied, "When I saw that the men were scattering, and that you did not come at the set time, and that the Philistines were assembling at Mikmash, I thought, 'Now the Philistines will come down against me at Gilgal, and I have not sought the LORD's favor.' So I felt compelled to offer the burnt offering." "You have done a foolish thing," Samuel said. "You have not kept the command the LORD your God gave you; if you had, he would have established your kingdom over Israel for all time. But now your kingdom will not endure; the LORD has sought out a man after his own heart and appointed him ruler of his people, because you have not kept the LORD's command. (NIV)

When Saul was confronted by Samuel, he made excuses for his actions and tried to blame others. As a result, God rejected him. In desperation Saul sought the advice from a witch, according to the Scriptures.

> Samuel said, "Why do you consult me, now that the Lord has departed from you and become your enemy? The Lord has done what he predicted through me. The Lord has torn the kingdom out of your hands and given it to one of your neighbors to David. Because you did not obey the Lord or carry out his fierce wrath against the Amalekites,

the Lord has done this to you today. The Lord will deliver both Israel and you into the hands of the Philistines, and tomorrow you and your sons will be with me. The Lord will also give the army of Israel into the hands of the Philistines." Immediately Saul fell full length on the ground, filled with fear because of Samuel's words. His strength was gone, for he had eaten nothing all that day and all that night. (1 Samuel 28:16–20 NIV)

These stories were written in the Bible, not for our entertainment but as guidelines for us to follow. Pastors and other religious leaders are held to a higher standard, and the Lord will not hesitate to deal with us. We are expected to live our lives as He commanded in His Word. We represent him in everything we do, so we must be careful not to discredit or besmirch His reputation. Since Christ no longer walks the earth, it is His intention for us to pick up where He left off by loving and caring for His sheep. But in order for us to carry out His will, we must be like Him.

It is futile to be Christian leaders trying to win souls for the kingdom when we are not living right. Ungodly lifestyles will cause the secular world to lose respect for the Word of God; they will also cause observers to have no interest in becoming followers of Christ. Not only that, but on that day, we will have to give account for the many times we took matters in our hands and overrode the Word. Second Corinthians 5:10 says, "For we must all appear before the judgment seat of Christ, so that each of us may receive what is due us for the things done while in the body, whether good or bad" (NIV).

CHAPTER 2

Spiritual Abuse

Those who desire to serve God as elders desire a
good thing. But the desire alone is never enough.
This desire must be accompanied by moral
character and spiritual capacity.

—Benjamin Merkle

To begin with, spiritual abuse is bad. Since it *is* bad, it is obviously
not from God because He has only good intentions for us, as
evidenced in the Scriptures. Jeremiah 29:11 says, "'For I know the
plans I have for you,' declares the LORD, 'plans to prosper you and
not to harm you, plans to give you hope and a future'" (NIV).

God will never do anything or allow anything or anyone to
harm His children. Since it has been established that spiritual abuse
is bad and not from God, it is now safe to say that it is from the Devil.
Things and situations are either good or bad. They are either from
the Lord or from the Devil, and there are no in-betweens. I believe
I am correct in saying that this is something that God did not give
or did not intend for us to have and to entertain. Oftentimes we
tend to do or say certain things in the name of Jesus, when Jesus did
not give us the authority to do so. We assume that since we serve a
loving and understanding God who is kind and patient, surely He
won't mind how we use His name, surely He would understand.

This is one of the many areas where we find ourselves in spiritual hot water. Some important rules to follow are:

1. If God did not tell you to say it, don't say it.
2. If God did not tell you to do it, don't do it.
3. If God did not give it to you, don't take it. *Give it back!*

It was not intended for you; walk in your calling and be satisfied where the Lord placed you. He did not give us permission to use and abuse anyone. He never did, and never will, so get rid of that attitude now. We should not use Christ's name in ways to support our self-interests and egotistical lifestyles; God sees them and He doesn't approve.

Some male church leaders are under the impression that women were created to do whatever they ask. The same applies to the female church leaders who believe that the man was fashioned to obey their commands. They have twisted the words of God in order to satisfy their selfish needs and then have attempted to validate their deeds by quoting the Scriptures. There is no place in the Scriptures where God instructed His leaders and elders to belittle, condemn, or depreciate anyone. Even in cases where we may think that certain individuals are worthy of such treatment, Christ never badmouthed or trash talked anyone. A perfect example is found in the story about the woman at the well. John 4:7–9 says, "When a Samaritan woman came to draw water, Jesus said to her, 'Will you give me a drink?' [His disciples had gone into the town to buy food.]The Samaritan woman said to him, 'You are a Jew and I am a Samaritan woman. How can you ask me for a drink?'" [For Jews do not associate with Samaritans.]

In today's society, we probably would not have given this woman the time of day, but God saw something else in her. Ordinary people like us would've reprimanded that woman and probably chased her away from Jesus, which most likely would have pushed her further into sin. But our compassionate Father saw beyond her mess and showed her love; as a result, not only a new babe in Christ was born, but she was able to save others by sharing the good news with others.

In His short time on earth, Christ was all about respect and treating others with admiration, and He encouraged us to do the same. Philippians 2:3 says, "Let nothing be done through strife or vain glory; but in lowliness of mind let each esteems other better than themselves" (KJV). Christ, in all his wisdom, knew that there would be misunderstandings, so He inspired Peter to warn us in 1 Peter 3:7, "Likewise, husbands, live with your wives in an understanding way, showing honor to the woman as the weaker vessel, since they are heirs with you of the grace of life, so that your prayers may not be hindered."

During His ministry on earth, He always encouraged everyone to love. It is not His intention that anyone be harmed, so it is difficult to understand why this and the other forms of abuse are alive, well, and going unnoticed in so many households and churches. This is because of the Devil's subtle forms of approach. He introduced this sin in a manner that is sly, cunning, and not easily noticeable. This dreadful crime infiltrates the lives of believers in a conniving way; it sneaks upon us like a slow leak. And before long, we are unintentionally and subconsciously entertaining it. Who knows? Maybe one who is reading this book at this very moment is a victim and not even aware of it.

The objective of this writing is not to cause confusion and disturbance in the homes or churches. Instead, it is intended to let people become aware of the signs and the causes of this abuse. Its purpose is to educate readers so that they will be aware of its existence. In that way they will learn more about it and be able to resist it and deal with it. It will also help to increase knowledge so that they will, in turn, educate their families. Then they will be able to enlighten others.

It appears that some spiritual leaders have placed themselves on their self-made pedestals. At the same time, they arrogantly position their spouses at their feet rather than by their sides. They request their partners to submit to their every whim. This is not a part of God's plan concerning His prized investments (His children), because He loves everyone equally and unconditionally. No one was given permission to use or abuse another. In fact, the Bible preaches the opposite.

John wrote in1 John 3:16–18, "This is how we know what love is: Jesus Christ laid down his life for us. And we ought to lay down our lives for our brothers. If anyone has material possessions and sees his brother in need but has no pity on him, how can the love of God be in him? Dear children, let us not love with words or tongue but with actions and in truth" (NIV).

First Peter 3:8 also says, "Finally, all of you, live in harmony with one another; be sympathetic, love as brothers, be compassionate and humble" And to the husbands He said "Husbands, love your wives, as Christ loved the church and gave himself up for her" (Ephesians 5:25). To both the wives and the husbands the apostle wrote, "Wives, submit to your own husbands, as to the Lord. For the husband is the head of the wife even as Christ is the head of the church, his body, and is himself its Savior. Now as the church submits to Christ, so also wives should submit in everything to their husbands. Husbands love your wives, as Christ loved the church and gave himself up for her, that he might sanctify her, having cleansed her by the washing of water with the word" (Ephesians 5:22–23 ESV).

Hebrew 13:4 also says, "Let marriage be held in honor among all, and let the marriage bed be undefiled, for God will judge the sexually immoral and adulterous" (ESV).

In addition to these Scriptures, there are so many more that encourage and enlighten us on how to live in love and unity. I include these to corroborate my statements about God's intentions for us. Christ, in His infinite wisdom, has a Scripture for everyone and every occasion, and each one is easily accessible. No one is omitted or forgotten, so when it comes to loving and caring for others, there is no excuse. Christian leaders must be found blameless and above reproach at all times. Warren Bennis says, "Leaders take charge, make things happen, dream dreams and then translate them into reality. Leaders attract the voluntary commitment of followers, energize them and transform organizations into new entities with greater potential for survival, growth and excellence."

Despite the fact that there are so many spiritual leaders whom God placed in positions of authority, there will always be sheep among us who will rely on us for spiritual guidance. Matthew 26:11 says, "The poor you will always have with you, but you will not always have me" (NIV). Another section of the Bible also says, "There will always be poor people in the land. Therefore I command you to be openhanded toward your fellow Israelites who are poor and needy in your land" (Deuteronomy 15:11).

The world has been faced with the ugly problem of poverty for thousands of years, but today most of us are dealing with it by looking the other way. I spoke to many people in the church who firmly believe that poverty is a result of laziness and people's foolish choices. That may be true for some people, but that should be no reason to refuse to help them. We make crazy mistakes daily, and our heavenly Father still gives us sunshine and rain. We may chose to ignore and try to forget about the poor, but God always remembers them, and He expects us to do the same. Notice most of His time on earth was spent catering to the poor, diseased, lame, and blind.

Christ was not only referring to the people who are monetarily poor and needy, but also those who are spiritually poor and needy. In other words, we are instructed to feed the people with physical food as well as spiritual food (the unalterable Word of God). That is why He blessed some of us with excess, not to spend it all on ourselves, but to accommodate those who are needy. Second Corinthians 9:8 says, "And God will generously provide all you need. Then you will always have everything you need and plenty left over to share with others" (NLT).

CHAPTER 3

Some of the Signs of Spiritual Abuse

> You may not be allowed to confront or question those in leadership as they are God's anointed. Members are taught that only God is to intervene in situations where leadership may have done wrong. (L. Gibson, 1997, par. 1).

We previously discussed the subtle ways that spiritual abuse can sneak up on God's people. It is therefore beneficial for our spiritual safety to be alert to its existence and learn to avoid it. I believe that as you read some of the signs mentioned and when you attend church services in the future, you will be able to identify any indications of spiritual abuse. Chances are that at first you may not see any signs or signals. You may not see signals at all, but if something is not right, eventually you will detect it.

I am not encouraging you to go to church to act as private investigators; nor am I encouraging you to become distracted as you look for signs of abuse in the church. The primary focus when attending church is to prepare to receive the Word. Then, if something is not right and you are following God's commandments, the Holy Spirit will speak to your heart. I merely want you to be educated about this demon's existence and the damage it is capable of inflicting. Here are some of the signs and symptoms of this type of abuse:

a. It is spiritual abuse when the congregation favors the pastor rather than establishing a personal relationship with God. Many churches worship their spiritual leaders to the point that they cannot function without them, when they should be focusing on God.

We must remember that bishops, pastors, elders, and other leaders are all aspiring to be like Christ, which means no one is perfect. We all are humans with mortal limitations; we are imperfect, limited, and inadequate. There is only one who is perfect and that is Jesus Christ and our Christian relationship should be solely with Him. So as you attend your church of preference on your worship days, please be sure to establish a personal relationship with God, not with the pastor or any church leader. If your leader is called home to heaven, do not lose your faith or feel sad, angry, or guilty; instead, rest assured that the Lord will provide another of His servants to replace the one He called home. The work of the Lord must be continued at all times, and at all costs. As 1 Chronicles 28:20 says, "Then David said to Solomon his son, 'Be strong and courageous and do it. Do not be afraid and do not be dismayed, for the Lord God, even my God, is with you. He will not leave you or forsake you, until all the work for the service of the house of the Lord is finished.'" (KJV).

b. It is considered spiritual abuse if the pastor teaches, heals, and preaches as if he or she is Jesus Christ, Himself.

Some of us probably can sing like archangels, preach like Paul, or are able to recite the verses in the Bible from Genesis to Revelation, but that is as far as we can go. Everything we do is all superficial; there is no depth in our words. I am here to remind you of the important fact that we don't know it all, and we can't do it all, because after all, we are not Christ. All the answers are in the hands of our heavenly Father, who is so wise that He withheld certain revelations from us. If He had not done that, maybe he would be sharing the kingdom with Satan at this very moment because Satan would have known too much and probably would have thought he was in charge. There is obviously no comparison to the King of Kings, and Lord of Lords. We are nothing compared to our heavenly Father; He is all-seeing, all-knowing, and almighty. So for those of us who believe that we are on the same level as God or equal to Him, think again! This belief is reflected in the actions of people who are saturated with pride and arrogance. Jeremiah 6:13–14 says, "From the least to the greatest, all are greedy for gain; prophets and priests alike, all practice deceit. They dress the wound of my people as though it were not serious. 'Peace, peace,' they say, when there is no peace" (NIV).

We must beware of imitators who daily walk this earth seeking to confuse and bamboozle God's servants. Pastor Mike Fehlauer of the Tree of Life Church in New Braunfels, says, "A healthy church should produce peace and rest for your soul. Establishing healthy spiritual relationships will always be a challenge, but the process will prevent you from becoming weary and worn, trying to jump through religious hoops that promise God's acceptance and love. If, in order to gain the acceptance of its leaders, your church constantly requires more and more of your life with no end in sight and little encouragement along the way then you may want to re-examine the church you are attending." (2001, par.16).

When it comes to the blessings of God, they were not only meant for the leaders but for all of us. We cannot spend every moment of our three or four hours in church stroking the pastor's ego and then leave church feeling drained. We are supposed to be our brother's keeper, bearing one another's burdens, and lifting each other up in prayer. Remember that whatever our status in the church, from the usher to the overseer, our heavenly Father loves and cares for us. He never puts His people in different classes or groups; He doesn't love us according to our ranks or by how well we dress. In fact, His ministry through Christ was all about serving rather than being served. Mark 10:42–45 says, "And Jesus called them to him and said to them, 'You know that those who are considered rulers of the Gentiles lord it over them and their great ones exercise authority over them. But it shall not be so among you. But whoever would be great among you must be your servant, and whoever would be first among you must be slave of all. For even the Son of Man came not to be served but to serve, and to give his life as a ransom for many." (ESV).

c. It is spiritual abuse when a pastor believes that the church is his or her property and that he or she is the boss and therefore is solely in charge.

The church is God's house where His people are free to come together and worship in love and unity. Romans 12:3–5 says, "For by the grace given me I say to every one of you: Do not think of yourself more highly than you ought, but rather think of yourself with sober judgment, in accordance with the measure of faith God has given you. Just as each of us has one body with many members, and these members do not all have the same function, so in Christ we who are many form one body, and each member belongs to all the others." (NIV).

We are all important to God who created us. There are no levels of love for us because He loves us all equally and unconditionally. God does not love one person because the individual is lighter or darker in skin color or because he or she has longer or shorter hair. There is no partiality when it comes to the love He has for us. Whether we are good or bad, rich or poor, He loves us all and provides for us equally. The Scripture says, "That ye may be the children of your Father which is in heaven: for he maketh his sun to rise on the evil and on the good, and sendeth rain on the just and on the unjust" (Matthew 5:45 KJV). So as Christians, we must regard each other as equals and friends, the way God recognizes us.

d. It is spiritual abuse when a minister preaches and encourages love and unity in the pulpit, yet at home, his wife and children are terrified of him.

Jesus' message to Peter is clear. Loving Him means caring for ("feeding") His little ones ("lambs"). On the surface, the church seems to have remembered this. The manicured lawns, smiling faces, and open arms of greeting at church doors could be an inviting alternative to the rugged way of life offered in a society of corporate cataclysms and *survival of the fittest* mentality. People are looking for acceptance, stability, even guidance. Ultimately they're looking for God, and the church should be the end of this search. (See G. Bloomer, p. 15.)

Spiritual leaders, love the ministry that God has entrusted in your care; at the same time, love your spouse the way God loves us. Anything contrary to this is hypocritical and therefore not of God. Gary Chapman says, "Dominant personalities are goal-oriented, not relationship-oriented. They get things done, but they hurt people in the process." (Chapman, 2008, p. 90).

It is the same as a member who is so anointed and speaks in different *tongues* on church day, yet the individual and his or her neighbor are not on speaking terms. Or the individual who appears to be so spiritually grounded and yet does not like his or her fellow singers in the choir. These are the actions of hypocrites, and the Lord is definitely not pleased. Titus 1:10–11 says, "For there are many who are insubordinate, empty talkers and deceivers, especially those of the circumcision party. They must be silenced, since they are upsetting whole families by teaching for shameful gain what they ought not to teach." (ESV).

e. It is spiritual abuse when a controlling pastor informs the members of the church that they will not receive God's blessings if they leave the church.

Craig Von Buseck says, "When a pastor tells the congregation that those who leave the church or disobey his authority are in danger of God's wrath, you can be sure this man is operating in a spirit of control. He is attempting to sow fear as a carnal means of keeping people in his church." (Von Buseck, 2015, par. 3).

I recall some years ago, a certain church member decided to

leave the place where he worshipped and began to fellowship at another sanctuary. It happened that about a year after the transition, the individual passed away. The pastor seized that opportunity to inform his congregation that the man's death was as a result of disobedience because he abandoned the church. What that pastor actually did was sow seeds of fear into his members just so they would remain faithful to the church. First John 4:18 says, "There is no fear in love. But perfect love drives out fear, because fear has to do with punishment. The one who fears is not made perfect in love." (First John 4:18, NIV).

f. It is also spiritual abuse and a shame when church leaders manipulate the congregation into believing that the more money they give to the church, the more blessings they will receive in their health and their wealth.

In other words, they are leading their congregations to believe that they can buy their ways to heaven. As a result of these false teachings, people have been known to give their mortgage payments, their car payments, and utility bill payments to their pastors, knowing that their bills are soon or past due. They willingly do this because they are led to believe that their money (as well as their blessings) will be doubled or tripled. I want everyone to know that this is not true; there is no doubt that our provider is able to bless us in extraordinary ways, and when He does He will reveal it to us. It is clear that whatever God gives us is free of charge, there are no conditions attached. He fills us with wisdom to know when to give, and how to give. It was quite evident that this pastor and many others are on missions in which only self and greed were involved.

An experience at a church anniversary showed the pastor asking the congregation to sow seeds of $1000 in support of his ministry. The sermon was put on hold because, according to the pastor, he was aware that God gave the people the funds to put into the plate, but they were being disobedient. He stated that he would hold up the service until the people did what the Lord told them to do. He also claimed that God gave him the names of the people who were required to *bless* his ministry, and planned to *expose* them if they refused to give willingly. Before long, the members reluctantly walked to the front of the church with their checkbooks. It was obvious that even though they walked toward the altar, most of them were not able to give the amount requested. So the pastor suggested that the people be divided into two rows. One of the rows was for those who were able to donate $500 and the other for those who were able to donate $1000. The sermon was put on hold for so long that some people attempted to leave, but surprisingly, the pastor instructed the two burly ushers in the back to secure the exits so no one could leave. Despite the ushers' persistence, the frustrated people excused themselves and exited the building.

This is one of many ways that believers are experiencing the effects of spiritual abuse because church services have become auction events. Attending church services should always be inspiring and exciting experiences. One should not feel threatened or inferior in any way, but instead, should feel the love of God. Parishioners should not be prompted to give more than what they are able to contribute. The pursuit of money should not be the pastor's top priority. Joseph Bush Jr. says, "Part of our vocation as clergy is to encourage virtuous character in persons and to labor for just systems and procedures in institutions." (Bush, Jr., 2006, p. 51).

In the Scriptures Paul was not happy with those who are in the ministry in order to make money. They twist God's Word in order to deceive His people. Romans 16:18 says, "For such people are not serving our Lord Christ, but their own appetites. By smooth talk and flattery they deceive the minds of naive people." (NIV).

I recall where the Lord instructed Peter to feed His sheep, not rob them. For these people are not serving our Lord Christ, but they are feeding their own appetites. Through smooth talk and flattery they deceive the minds of naive people.

"The thought is disgusting, but it is happening all the time, and it's time we started pointing it out and objecting to the commercial corruption of the pulpit. While a lot of deserved attention is being paid these days to the deceptive marketing behind many celebrity pastors' books, another aspect of the whole endeavor reveals the primacy of commercial interests." Duncan, J., 2015, par. 2).

g. It is definitely spiritual abuse when the female leader in the church takes her authority to the extreme.

This individual has a tendency to take her position to another level, which is outside the will of God. This is what is referred to by some as the *Jezebel spirit*. Look for Jezebel to target women who are embittered against men, either through neglect or misuse of authority. This spirit operates through women who, because of insecurity, jealousy, or vanity, desire to dominate others. The Jezebel spirit is there behind the woman who publicly humiliates her husband with her tongue and thereafter controls him by his fear of public embarrassment. (See Frangipane, F. p. 9.)

"A person operating in the spirit of witchcraft focuses conversations around themselves. They want to talk about them, them, them and them." (Jonas, C., 2011, p. 2). Remember that the Devil's plan is to destroy our lives and discourage us from continuing the work of God. And he will stop at nothing to accomplish his plan, especially since he knows that his fate is already sealed. So, because we have hope that gives us reasons to persevere, we must fight back. I don't mean fist fighting with guns and other weapons. Since it is a spiritual battle, we must resort to using spiritual tools in order to be victorious. I know that some of us are pumped up and physically strong, but without spiritual strength, it profits nothing. With no time spent before the Lord and not reading our Bibles, our battles will be totally hopeless, and we will die spiritual deaths. Being physically fit, with every internal organ working efficiently and every muscle in place, we are still not strong enough to resist the Devil and hell. The Holy Bible consists of many Scriptures that teach us how to fight these spiritual battles. Second Corinthians 10:3–5 says, "For though we live in the world, we do not wage war as the world does. The weapons we fight with are not the weapons of the world. On the contrary, they have divine power to demolish strongholds. We demolish arguments and every pretension that sets itself up against the knowledge of God, and we take captive every thought to make it obedient to Christ." (NIV).. Ephesians 6:10–17 says,

> Finally, be strong in the Lord and in his mighty power. Put on the full armor of God, so that you can take your stand against the devil's schemes. For our struggle is not against flesh and blood, but against the rulers, against the authorities, against the powers of this dark world and against the spiritual forces of evil in the heavenly realms. Therefore put on the full armor of God, so that when the day of evil comes, you may be able to stand your ground, and after you have done everything, to stand. Stand firm then, with the belt of truth buckled around your waist, with the breastplate of righteousness in place, and with your feet fitted with the readiness that comes from the gospel of peace. In addition to all this, take up the shield of faith, with which you can extinguish all the flaming arrows of the evil one. Take the helmet of salvation and the sword of the Spirit, which is the word of God. (NIV)

h. It is also considered spiritual abuse when Christian leaders who are placed in authority abuse those who are entrusted in their care.

Pastor Andy Stanley tells a story about a little boy who was scolded by his mother because he refused to share his lunch with a classmate who had brought no lunch to school that day. The ironic point, Stanley says, is that we expect our children to know that possessions are for sharing, yet when it comes to our own affairs, we act as if possessions are for keeping. But why else, according to the Bible, should we give? First, we should give because it is a reasonable response to all God has done. Because God has shown such great mercy to His people by sending Christ to suffer in our place. (See R. Harp, par. 1.)

When there is a shortage of food and people are hungry, it becomes very difficult to minister to them about the love of God. In the Scriptures we read the story about Jesus feeding the multitudes, both spiritually and physically. According to Mark, chapter 8, He fed them with seven loaves and a few small fish. "During those days another large crowd gathered. Since they had nothing to eat, Jesus called his disciples to him and said, 'I have compassion for these people; they have already been with me three days and have nothing to eat. If I send them home hungry, they will collapse on the way, because some of them have come a long distance'" (NIV).

This is the same principle He wants us to adapt to today. Mahatma Gandhi was quoted, "There are people in the world so hungry, that God cannot appear to them except in the form of bread."(Van Schooneveld, A., 2010, par. 3). It is always nice to go to church on your day of worship, but not to return to a home without food to eat. Christ lived His life teaching us how to be good stewards, and if at any time we become confused, we can always go back to the manual, which is the Holy Bible.

This unpleasant experience in the church has opened my eyes to one of the many ways that God's people are hurting and disappointed with Christians, causing them to subsequently walk away from the church. Our actions are the main reasons why so many people are working for the Devil. He certainly has no problem hiring, and he also promised great benefits. I cringe with embarrassment when I listen to some of their reasons for not attending church.

a. "Church people are evil."
b. "They worship money more than anything else."
c. "Church folks deal with witchcraft."
d. "They have too many offering plates."
e. "What's going on with that building fund box? It is never full."
f. "Church people? Wicked, wicked, wicked."
g. "No disrespect, but I don't do business with church people."
h. "When I go to church, I do not feel welcome. I feel out of place."
i. "They love money more than the gospel."

This is one of those delicate moments when I do not have proper responses to these people who seem so angry with us. The same people whom Christ commissioned us to reach are disappointed with us. This makes me realize that the battle is far from over and that we have more work to do.

The Devil will stop at nothing to get his grip on God's precious investments. This means that everyone needs to learn that no matter how safe we think we are from evil, we are not impervious to the Devil's schemes. If we are not careful, we too will fall. Many pastors are using treachery and deceitfulness to enslave God's people, and they use the Word of God to validate they plans. Stephen Arterburn and Jack Felton say, "Many believers struggle to find a real relationship with God because their groups, rules, regulations, and religious rituals become the main focus in their lives, displaying a powerful and personal God. They grow blind to practices that misplace faith in faith structure, false leaders, good works and many other spiritual substitutes. Such false practices have the scent and feel of God, but they lack His holy presence." (Arteburn/Felton, 2001).

One important thing we must understand about the Devil is that he is very fashion-conscious. He is hip to the latest fashions. He knows every language, and he is able to blend in to every culture.

He knows how to dress to impress God's people, especially their children. When it comes to studying the lives of Christians, he is dedicated to the cause of destroying us. He is always one step ahead of us, and because we lack wisdom, he knows where we are going before we even get there. I am certainly not here to boost his ego but to give you an idea of how dedicated he is to his mission. In the same way, we can all put our differences aside, come together in unity, and fight.

CHAPTER 4

Ways to Overcoming Spiritual Abuse

> Those of us who walked the path of deception are
> uniquely able to relate to one another. For some
> trust become virtually impossible after confronting
> deception of our past. Others do not want to set
> foot in another church because they are hurt and
> angry. We react to our wounds differently, but
> we are all keenly aware of how difficult it is for
> other Christians to understand or relate to our
> experiences. I want to help those who are hurting
> and lacking the emotional support they need to
> find healing. While I cannot personally reach out
> to every hurting person, I can educate.
>
> (Shari Howerton, Charlie Daniels, 2001).

As with any other type of abuse, the recovery process is not an easy
task. It takes dedication and perseverance to defeat spiritual abuse.
I am not a doctor or a therapist, but I believe that my experiences
have both taught me the importance of sharing my story with those
who have had similar experiences and with those who are not fully
aware of the existence of spiritual abuse.

There is a great urgency to get the gospel to everyone because
this war gets more intense each day. And, if we are not fully armored
spiritually, chances are that we will lose not only this battle, but

many more to come. The chance of losing battles to the Devil should not be among our list of options. The Scriptures say that we are "more than conquerors." We must always be on high alert because the Devil is very cunning. We never know what scheme he is planning, when his next attack will be, or what route he will take. The Scripture says, "Be alert and of sober mind. Your enemy the devil prowls around like a roaring lion looking for someone to devour. Resist him, standing firm in the faith, because you know that the family of believers throughout the world is undergoing the same kind of sufferings (1 Peter 5:8–9 NIV). It's important to know that, in order to be successful in these spiritual battles, we must be spiritually fit. Building up one's physical self will not help in this type of war because it is a spiritual conflict. Billy Graham says, "We live in a perpetual battlefield. The wars among the nations on earth are mere popgun affairs compared to the fierceness of battle in the spiritual unseen world. This invisible spiritual conflict is waged around us incessantly and unremittingly. Where the Lord works, Satan's forces hinder; where angel beings carry out divine directives, the devils rage. All this comes about because the powers of darkness press their counterattack to recapture the ground held for the glory of God." (Graham, 2015, par. 2).

This warfare is real, and as long as we are living and working for the Lord, we will always have conflict with the Enemy. We will be free from this spiritual warfare when the Lord calls His people home. So let us inform our fellow Christians about the damages of spiritual abuse.

A large percentage of the people interviewed were not aware of spiritual abuse, and they are entertaining it even as we speak. In the words of the holocaust historian Yehuda Bauer, "Thou shall not be a perpetrator; thou shall not be a victim; and thou shall never but never be a bystander." (Bauer, 2014, par. 14).

One of Satan's tactics is to infiltrate the church, and what easier way to do it than to attack and divide the family. His plan is to attack and destroy the head of the home and the church, and then it will become easier for him to destroy the body. In the book of Genesis, remember when the deceiver (Satan) visited the Garden of Eden. The purpose of that trip was not to marvel at God's handiwork nor was it to admire the zebra's stripes or the leopard's spots. He did not show up to get decorating tips from the Creator. I believe that his main purpose was to annihilate God's plans by destroying the one who was placed in authority, Adam. It is the same way he is operating in the churches today—by attacking the church leaders and husbands.

I believe that the time has come when this swindler and liar must be exposed for the conniving individual he really is. Now is the time when we should not be afraid to confront him with the power that the Lord gives us. Beth Moore tweeted, "The richest testimonies come from people whom Christ has made whole and who still remember what it was like to be broken." (Moore, 2006, p. 26).

I believe that there are thousands of people today who are not affiliated with the church, because of the spiritual and other kinds of abuse they have suffered. We must speak up to let them know that Christ is loving and caring and has no intention of harming them. It is also important that they understand that not everyone who professes to be a Christian is a true follower of Christ. Show these disaffected ones the Scriptures that warn against false leaders. One such Scripture is Matthew 7:15, which says, "Beware of false prophets which come to you in sheep's clothing but inwardly they are ravening wolves." (KJV). Second Corinthians 11:13–15 adds, "For such are false apostles, deceitful workers, transforming themselves into the apostles of Christ. And no marvel; for Satan himself is transformed into an angel of light. Therefore it is no great thing if his ministers also be transformed as the ministers of righteousness; whose end shall be according to their works." (KJV).

We must inform those outside of the church that the lifestyle of a Christian is a wonderful experience, where our heavenly Father loves us unconditionally and cares for us. We must show them through our lifestyles that a life with Christ is the most important relationship anyone could possibly have. Martin Padovani says, "Religion is supposed to bring peace, joy, hope, comfort, consolation. It is supposed to help alleviate life's misery, not add to it. Why then do so many suffer torment, agony, anxiety and senseless guilt about their religion? Why do religious people experience misery from religion?" (Padovani, 2006, p. 133).

It does not matter what situations we are in, or whether we are believers or not; the gospel is for everyone. The Lord hates when we are divided, especially for petty reasons such as another's way of singing or teaching. He hates it when we nitpick and find fault with one another. In an article written by Dave Bookless, "The famous Indian poet and playwright Rabindranath Tagore was once asked why, despite a deep admiration for Jesus, he never considered becoming a Christian. He replied, 'On that day when we see Jesus Christ living out His life in you, on that day we Hindus will flock to your Christ even as doves flock to their feeding ground.'" (Bookless, 2008).

Does this statement tell you that we have work to do? I hope so! Too much time is wasted fighting against one another in the faith, when in fact we should all come together for the common good, which is to defeat Satan. We must declare spiritual war on the Enemy, break down all dividing walls, and become united with one another. We are the ones standing in the way of sinners with our stupidity and insanity. The Scripture says, "Not so the wicked! They are like chaff that the wind blows away. Therefore the wicked will not stand in the judgment, nor sinners in the assembly of the righteous." (Psalm 1:4–5). We cannot wave the white flag and throw in the towel; instead, God wants us to rise up from our spiritual slumber, and march on as soldiers going to war (NIV). Bishop T. D. Jakes says,

> Warring in the spirit is much more than standing
> up from time to time telling the Devil to stop

hindering our finances or making us sick. Warring in the spirit is defeating all the little foxes that would spoil the vine, little foxes such as greed, lust, jealousy, anger and fear. Warring in the spirit is getting up an hour early, or staying up an hour later to have that intimate time with the Lord, to hear His instructions for the day, to know his heart and mind, to be empowered with His might, and to be fully clothed in His armor so that the enemy will be driven farther back as we walk in this world (Jakes, 2000).

Mr. Preston Bailey also had something to say about this. "Christian soldiers are not to sit quietly while Satan tries to destroy the world and the kingdom of God. We are to resist him with the power of God and not our own strength. Satan is not scared of us. But he is frightened by the Omnipotent power of God." (Bailey, 2008).

Christ wants us to stand together in unity and fight so we can be effective soldiers. In order for the battle to be successful, our lives must be aligned with the Word of God. It is quite obvious how the Enemy slithers into our intimate spaces such as our homes, which is a sign that we must get it together before he takes it from us.

C. S. Lewis says, "The Christian way is different: harder, and easier. Christ says 'Give me All. I don't want so much of your time and so much of your money and so much of your work: I want you. I have not come to torment your natural self, but to kill it. No half-measures are any good. I don't want to cut off a branch here and a branch there, I want the whole tree down. I don't want to drill the tooth or crown it, or stop it, but to have it out.'" (Lewis, 1980).

So let us get right by equipping ourselves with the armor of God and boldly march into battle. The signs show clearly that we are asleep, with our spiritual lamps untrimmed and without oil. We are so dead spiritually that we are not even aware that the Devil and his followers have moved into our homes and our churches and set up shop. Dr. Ralph Curtin couldn't have said it better, "The church must be awakened in order to defeat the enemy bent on destroying the divinely ordained custodian of faith and truth – the Church." (Curtin, 2009, p. 161). He further stated, "As long as the church sleeps at the post, disunity abounds and the war cannot be won" (Curtin, 2009,p. 161).

So let us armor ourselves and go to war and restore our homes and our churches; because whether we like it or not, whether we are prepared or not, the war has begun. As Sabine Baring-Gould wrote the encouraging words of this song:

> Onward, Christian soldiers, marching as to war,
> With the cross of Jesus going on before.
> Christ, the royal Master, leads against the foe;
> Forward into battle see His banners go!
> At the sign of triumph Satan's host doth flee;
> On then, Christian soldiers, on to victory!
> Hell's foundations quiver at the shout of praise;
> Brothers lift your voices, loud your anthems raise.
> Refrain
> Onward, Christian soldiers, marching as to war,
> With the cross of Jesus going on before.

In my research I came across a very interesting book, *Near to the Heart of God* by Robert J. Morgan. I was impressed with a touching story he wrote.

> On Tuesday, March 30, 1858, Rev. Dudley Tyng, age twenty-nine, addressed a mass gathering of men in Philadelphia, exhorting them to serve the Lord with all their hearts. "I would rather that this right arm was amputated at the trunk," he said, "than that I should come short of my duty

to you in delivering God's message." A week later in a freak accident, Tyng's arm was caught in the cogs of a corn thrasher and he was fatally injured. His dying words were, "Let us all stand up for Jesus." The following Sunday, Tyng's friend and fellow clergyman, George Duffield, preached from Ephesians 6:14, ending his sermon by reciting this poem he'd written for the occasion (Morgan, 2010).

Stand up, stand up for Jesus! Ye soldiers of the cross;
Lift high His royal banner, it must not suffer loss:
From victory unto victory, His army shall He lead,
Till every foe is vanquished, and Christ is Lord
    indeed.
Stand up, stand up for Jesus! The trumpet call obey:
Forth to the mighty conflict, in this His
    glorious day;
Ye that are men now serve Him against
    unnumbered foes;
Let courage rise with danger, and strength to
    strength oppose.
Stand up, stand up for Jesus! Stand in His strength
    alone,
The arm of flesh will fail you, ye dare not trust
    your own;
Put on the gospel armor, and watching unto prayer,
Where calls the voice of duty, be never wanting
    there.
Stand up, stand up for Jesus! The strife will not be
    long;
This day the noise of battle, the next the victor's
    song;
To him that overcometh a crown of life shall be;
He with the King of glory shall reign eternally.

> Stand therefore, having girded your waist
> with truth, having put on the breastplate of
> righteousness. (Ephesians 6:14, NKJV).

I must inform you that spiritual abuse is not Satan's only way to attack. He has hundreds, maybe thousands, of ways to infiltrate our lives. So while we are hard at work trying to resist him from one area, he and his followers are busily advancing from other directions. I believe it is important for me to tell you this because we are all at war with the Devil. There is not one person living on earth who does not have encounters with him. Whether we are rich or poor, black or white, man or woman, we've all been introduced to this demon at one point or another in our lives. So the only way we can battle and be successful is to submit our lives to God. James 4:7 says, "Submit yourselves therefore to God. Resist the devil, and he will flee from you" (NKJV).

I am also cautioning you that since you now understand something about spiritual abuse and how God can deliver you from this dreadful sin, it does not mean that you will be at peace. Satan is not done with you yet; in fact, the battle has just started because the Devil desperately wants you back. But this time he is not returning alone. Matthew 12:43–45 says, "When an impure spirit comes out of a person, it goes through arid places seeking rest and does not find it. Then it says, 'I will return to the house I left.' When it arrives, it finds the house unoccupied, swept clean and put in order. Then it goes and takes with it seven other spirits more wicked than itself, and they go in and live there. And the final condition of that person is worse than the first. That is how it will be with this wicked generation" (NIV). So it is important for all Christians to submit themselves wholly to Christ so that, even if the Devil tries to attack them, he won't succeed.

I decided to write about this issue because of my years of living the spiritually abusive lifestyle without being aware of it. I lived it comfortably for so long that even when help arrived, I refused any form of treatment because I thought I was doing very well. But that is how the Devil operates; he tries to convince us that everything is okay. Some of you are probably experiencing the same thing right now. But please understand that God is our Creator, not man. You and I are not the property of any man or woman. We were not mass produced to become anyone's possessions, but instead, we were individually and lovingly created by our Father. He intends for us to live in love and unity.

For those who are committed to one another in marriage, God wants couples to get the full understanding of His purpose and His love. He explains it clearly in the Scriptures. First Corinthians 11:3 says, "But I want you to realize that the head of every man is Christ, and the head of the woman is man, and the head of Christ is God." (NIV).

> Marriage is to be a union of man and woman, which teaches the many lessons God means for mankind to realize. Our flaws, faults, phobias, and many other human weaknesses cause us great distress in this life, and marriage often reflects that distress. But God intends that we learn the needed lessons and strive to live within His guidance. When humans love God and keep His commandments, they are strengthened and thus able to overcome the areas of life that are contrary to God. Living within the marriage covenant is a vital part of this understanding. I hasten to add that being married is not a requirement for salvation, and it is clear that not all people can marry (Berendt, R., 2002, par. 5).

Today there are many spiritual abusers in the churches who are doing, (according to them) the *will of God*. Some of their favorite phrases I've heard over the years are:

"Touch not the Lord's anointed."

"God chose me as your spiritual covering."

"If you disobey me, you disobey God."

"It's settled, no if's, and's or but's."

"God speaks to me every day."

"I know what I am doing."

"If you walk away from this church, you will surely die."

"I am in charge, not you."

"If you need prayer, come to me, because I am the one with the connection."

"God placed me as your boss for the home and the church, and what I say goes."

"If you disobey your spouse, you will have to answer to God."

These are some of the abusive attitudes that church members endure on a daily basis. It is sad to know that many of these abusive people are currently living respectable lives. They are probably preaching, healing, baptizing, encouraging, and leading others to Christ. Some have even written bestselling books teaching others how to live godly lives. Some have gone on to become celebrities, appearing in movies, on television talk shows, and on the radio.

It can become quite difficult and painful for the victims to watch such individuals being accepted by the world and sometimes being given great recognitions for doing great things. Yet the demon is still occupying major parts of their lives. They present a united front by smiling in front of the cameras, but behind closed doors they become their natural selves. God hates to see His reputation being tarnished by those deceivers, and guess what? The day is coming when they will have to answer to a higher authority.

This reminds me of the story of King David, who was a well-liked, well-respected leader and a man who walked after God's own heart. Yet he schemed, lied, committed adultery, and subsequently murdered Bathsheba's husband, Uriah. He went even further by attempting to cover up his crimes, which led him into more problems.

The Bible did not state how long these shenanigans lasted, but I presume that David went about his daily business as if everything was alright. He probably held many revivals and conferences; he probably offered sacrifices on behalf of others. David probably prayed over and blessed many people. Yet the evil deed was still not addressed; the sinful wound was covered with a Band Aid and started festering. He woke up every day and went about his daily routine as if everything was alright. If it had not been for the Prophet Nathan, whom the Lord sent to expose David's wound for everyone to see, the problem would not have been addressed.

Second Samuel 12:13–15 says, "So David said to Nathan, 'I have sinned against the Lord.' And Nathan said to David, 'The Lord also has put away your sin; you shall not die. However, because by this deed you have given great occasion to the enemies of the Lord to blaspheme, the child also *who is* born to you shall surely die.' Then Nathan departed to his house." (NKJV).

The Lord has His unique ways of exposing the sins of His people in His time. Until then, I encourage you to pray for the abusers and love them in spite of their deeds. We must also pray that their eyes will be opened to their evil ways so that they can change them before it is too late.

The Christian life is a wonderful experience that I would not trade for all the gold in Egypt. It is a great feeling when you belong to a family who loves and cares for you. God wants us, and He wants no misunderstanding where His love is concerned. Although His love is without price, most of us are still unlovable and so hard to break. We are so set in our ways, but He loves us anyway, which tells us about the heart of God. John 3:16–17 says, "For God so loved the world that he gave his only begotten Son, that whosoever believeth in him should not perish, but have everlasting life. For God sent not his Son into the world to condemn the world; but that the world through him might be saved" (KJV).

First Peter 2:9 also states, "But you are a chosen people, a royal priesthood, a holy nation, God's special possession, that you may declare the praises of him who called you out of darkness into his wonderful light" (NIV).

These and many, many more Scriptures are in the Bible as proof of God's love for us. In fact, it was because of His great love for us that He willingly went to the cross. That love cannot be compared to anything on earth.

Conclusion

As a survivor of spiritual abuse, this is my caution to everyone—
male or female—to be aware of spiritual abusers who will convince
you that you are their property. Be on guard and don't believe; it
is wrong and therefore sinful. After years of living this lifestyle,
it becomes so easy for one to believe that the woman was created
especially for the man to do whatever he pleases. One can also be
easily convinced that the woman's purpose on earth was solely
to please the man and to do whatever he says. After some time, it
becomes easy to accept one's circumstances and later become so
comfortable with the situation that it no longer appears to be an
issue.

It is very chauvinistic for one partner to teach the other to
submit to his or her demands. God intended for the woman to
be submissive to her husband, but it must be done respectfully
and lovingly. "For this is the way the holy women of the past who
put their hope in God used to adorn themselves. They submitted
themselves to their own husbands, like Sarah, who obeyed Abraham
and called him her lord. You are her daughters if you do what is
right and do not give way to fear" (1 Peter 3:5–6 NIV).

It is not amusing when church folks treat others in derogatory
ways and think that it is okay with God. Among the many things
that the church was called to do was to look out for the welfare
of its members; this is what being in fellowship is all about. It is
hypocritical to preach about love and respect in the church and

then sing a different tune in the home. Let us end this stupidity and thoughtlessness right now and concentrate on doing the work of our heavenly Father. While we are here wasting valuable time abusing each other, Satan and his organized armies are recruiting people for active duty in his army. Carolyn Custis -James makes it clear in her blog, "Combine individuals possessed of authority and power (who, as we noted last week, are often oblivious to their capacity for spiritual abuse) with individuals spiritually conditioned to submit to authority. Then add devotees/enablers who (out of a misguided sense of loyalty to the person in power and the desire to curry their favor) turn a blind eye to abusive behavior and may even defend it. Suddenly you have ideal conditions for spiritual abuse to bluster up and thrive unchecked." (Curtis-James, C., 2001).

Shari Howerton and Charlie Daniels also say, "Sometimes we must take a bold stand, accepting whatever personal consequences come as a result. Love and apathy cannot harmoniously coexist." (Howerton/Daniels, 2001).

Remember that when we choose to ignore what others are doing and pretend that things are okay (when in fact they are not) we are actually committing sinful acts. There are no first, second, or third classes of sin; a sin of any kind, no matter the severity, is a sin. James 2:10 says, "For whoever keeps the whole law but fails in one point has become accountable for all of it" (ESV).

So let us be our brother's keeper and be attentive to the needs of others. I thank God for the wisdom He has instilled in the lives of His people to write books or magazines on these and other delicate issues. People will always be mistreated in the church, but for each person who reads our books and learns from them, there will be one less person at risk for abuse I am praying for those who are ignorant to its existence and are still embracing this destructive spirit that they will eventually be delivered from that dreadful demon. Always remember that God's intention is for us to serve Him freely. It is not His will for any one of us to feel inferior or ashamed in any way. The apostle Paul encouraged us in these words:

For God has not given us a spirit of fear and timidity, but of power, love, and self-discipline. So never be ashamed to tell others about our Lord. And don't be ashamed of me, either, even though I'm in prison for him. With the strength God gives you, be ready to suffer with me for the sake of the Good News. For God saved us and called us to live a holy life. He did this, not because we deserved it, but because that was his plan from before the beginning of time—to show us his grace through Christ Jesus. And now he has made all of this plain to us by the appearing of Christ Jesus, our Savior. He broke the power of death and illuminated the way to life and immortality through the Good News. And God chose me to be a preacher, an apostle, and a teacher of this Good News. That is why I am suffering here in prison. But I am not ashamed of it, for I know the one in whom I trust, and I am sure that he is able to guard what I have entrusted to him until the day of his return. (2 Timothy 1:7–12 NLT)

Colossians 3:1–2 also says, "Since, then, you have been raised with Christ, set your hearts on things above, where Christ is, seated at the right hand of God. Set your minds on things above, not on earthly things." (NIV).

The Holy Book contains endless Scriptures that are very encouraging because our Father knew beforehand that there would be days like these. He knew that there would come a time when we would attempt to take matters into our own hands, and some of His children would be caught in the crossfire. Thank God for thinking of us long before we even came into existence.

To all those who will read this book, I pray that God will give you the wisdom to comprehend what you read, and you will, in turn, warn someone of the many dangers of spiritual abuse. Do not forget how much God loves you and wants only the best for you and me. You don't have to take my word for it; He inspired His servants to write encouraging words for us on our daily walk. Here are some of my favorite verses:

> **Zephaniah 3:17** The LORD your God is in your midst, a mighty one who will save; he will rejoice over you with gladness; he will quiet you by his love; he will exult over you with loud singing" (ESV).

> **1 John 4:7–8** "Beloved, let us love one another, for love is from God, and whoever loves has been born of God and knows God. Anyone who does not love does not know God, because God is love." (KJV).

> **John 3:16** "For God so loved the world, that he gave his only Son, that whoever believes in him should not perish but have eternal life." (ESV).

> **Romans 5:8** "But God shows his love for us in that while we were still sinners, Christ died for us." (ESV).

> **Deuteronomy 7:9** "Know therefore that the LORD your God is God, the faithful God who keeps covenant and steadfast love with those who love him and keep his commandments, to a thousand generations." (NIV).

> **Proverbs 8:17** "I love those who love me, and those who seek me diligently find me." (NIV).

Jeremiah 29:11 "For I know the plans I have for you, declares the LORD, plans for welfare and not for evil, to give you a future and a hope." (ESV).

Thank you for giving me this opportunity to share my experiences with you. I hope they will help you in your daily Christian walk. It is my prayer that you will share your new-found knowledge about spiritual abuse with others. May God bless and keep you always.

Some Questions for Your Personal Reflection

1. What is your personal opinion of spiritual abuse after reading this book?

   _____

   _____

   _____

   _____

   _____

2. I spoke to some people who believe that a clean house, well-behaved children, and a daily, home-cooked meal contribute to a peaceful, happy home. Do you believe that this is all that's needed in order to have a happy, peaceful home? If not, what are your reasons?

   _____

   _____

   _____

_____

_____

3. List some of the ways that you may be able to help someone
    who has experienced or is currently experiencing spiritual
    abuse.

_____

_____

_____

_____

_____

4. Are you living your life is an example for others to follow? If so,
    how are you making a difference?

_____

_____

_____

_____

_____

Sources

Arterburn, J., Felton, J. *Toxic Faith: Experience Healing Over Painful Spiritual Abuse*. Water Brook Press. Colorado Springs, CO. (2001).

Bailey, P. Jr. *Spiritual Warfare*. Zondervan Publishing House, Grand Rapids. MI. (2008).

Bauer, Y. Retrieved on 04/15/2014 from http://www.timeshigher education.co.uk/features/a-last-lesson-from-the-holocaust-thou-shalt-not-be-a-perpetrator-victim-or-a-bystander/168570. article. (2002).

Berendt, R. Retrieved on 05/21/2014 from http://www.ucg.org/relationships/gods-intent-marriage/ (2002).

Bloomer, G., *Authority Abusers*. Whitaker House, New Kensington, PA. (1984).

Bookless, D., Plantewise, *Dare to Care for God's World*. Intervarsity Press, Downers Grove, IL. (2008).

Bush Jr., J., *Gentle Shepherding, Pastoral Ethics & Leadership*. Hope Publishing Co., Carol Stream, IL. . (2006).

Chapman, G. *Desperate Marriages*. Northfield Publishing. Chicago, IL. (2008).

Clark, J., *How Witchcraft Spirits Attacks*. Spirit of Life Publishing. Hallandale, Fl. (2011).

Curtin, R. *Waking the Sleeping Church*. Lighthouse Christian Publishing. Savage, MI. (2009).

Curtis- James, C. Retrieved on 04/14/2014 from http://www.whitbyforum.com/2013/06/the-perfect-storm.html (2013).

Duncan, J., Retrieved on 05/19/2014 from http: //www.pajamapages.com/celebrity-pastors-are-selling-their-pulpits-for-commercial-gain/.(2014).

Fehlauer, M. *Exposing Spiritual Abuse*. Retrieved on 04/11/2014 from http://www.cbn.com/spirituallife/churchandministry/spiritual_abuse1.aspx (2001).

Frangipane, F., *The Jezebel Spirit*. Arrow Publications, Cedar Rapids, IA. (1977).

Graham, B., Retrieved on 05/14/2014 from http://www.battlefocused.org/spiritual-warfare/scriptures.php. (2014).

Henzel, R. Retrieved on 06/11/2014 from http://batteredsheep.com/bible_spiritual.html (2010).

Howerton, S., Daniels, C. *Breaking the Chains: Overcoming the Spiritual Abuse of a False Gospel*. Good News Publishers. Nashville, TN. (2001).

Gibson, L. Retrieved on 04/17/2014 from http://www.spiritualabuse. org/introduction.html. (1997).

Harp, R. Retrieved on 06/12/2014 from http://www.generouschurch. com/202. (2006).

Jakes, T.D. *Overcoming the Enemy.* Bethany House Publishers, Bloomington, MN.. (2000).

Lewis, C. *Mere Christianity.* Harper Collins Publishers. New York, NY. (1980).

Merkle, B. *40 Questions About Elders and Deacons.* Kregel Publications. Grand Rapids, MI. (2008).

Moore, B. *Praying God's Word Day by Day.* B & H Publishing Group. Nashville, TN. (2006).

Morgan, R. *Near to the Heart of God.* Baker Publishing Group. Grand Rapids, MI. (2010).

Padovani, M. *Healing Wounded Emotions: Overcoming Life's Hurts.* Twenty Third Publications, New London, CT.

Van Schooneveld, A., Retrieved on 03/26/2015 from http://www. relevantmagazine.com/reject-apathy/worldview/features/ 21690-god-in-the-form-of-bread. (2010).

Von Buseck, C., Retrieved on 04/23/2014 from www.cbn. com/spiritlife/BibleStudyAndTheology/Discipleship. VonBuseck_SpiritualAbuse.aspx (2012).

Van Vonderen, J., Ryan, D. *Soul Repair: Rebuilding Your Spiritual Life.* InterVarsity Press. Downers Grove, IL. (2008).

About the Author

 Yvonne Maxine Weir (born Yvonne Maxine Davis) was born on August 8, 1958 to Melbourne and Edith Davis in the beautiful island of Jamaica. There she attended three of the best schools, Park Hall Primary (Elementary) School, Frankfield High School in Frankfield, and Clarendon College, located in Chapelton. After graduating from high school, she enrolled in the nursing program for some years until 1980, when she and her son migrated to the United States. They lived in New Jersey for several years before moving to sunny Florida, where Yvonne continued her nursing profession. After the birth of her daughter, she decided to start her own business; that way she could bond with her children while simultaneously earning a living. She owned and operated the Little League Day Care Center for several years, which she later traded for her income tax and financial business still operating today.

While operating her business, Yvonne realized that her children were experiencing separation anxiety in school, so she became a volunteer in the public schools to be close to them during school hours. It was while volunteering that she met a very good friend who introduced her to Trinity International University. As a pastor Yvonne thought, *What better place to sharpen her pastoral skills than*

a Christian university? Not only did she become a more learned woman of God, but her other skills as a writer and poetess were stimulated. The birth of this book, as well as the other books, came about as a result of her enrollment at this university. The teaching and training she received at this school encouraged and inspired her to write several books.

Yvonne is currently pastoring at Rehoboth Outreach Center (R. O. C.) in Miami. She is also the founder and president of The Youth for Christ Foundation located in Miami.

Of all her achievements, she believes that her greatest accomplishments are her children: Michael, Linval, Sasha, Carlton Jr. (CJ), Samantha, and Clifford. She thanks God for them and pray that they will prosper in whatever they do.

Printed in the United States
By Bookmasters